Python Programming

for Beginners

How to Learn Python in Less Than One Week.

The Ultimate Step-by-Step Complete Course

from Novice to Advance Programmer

William Brown

reader will render any resulting actions solely under their purview. There are no scenarios in which the publisher or the original author of this work can be in any fashion deemed liable for any hardship or damages that may befall them after undertaking information described herein.

Additionally, the information in the following pages is intended only for informational purposes and should thus be thought of as universal. As befitting its nature, it is presented without assurance regarding its prolonged validity or interim quality. Trademarks that are mentioned are done without written consent and can in no way be considered an endorsement from the trademark holder.

Table of contents

Introduction

Most people thought about coding as a strange hobby for geeks who tinkered with machines in their basements. However, coding has evolved from a pastime to a necessary career ability in recent years. What's better for them hobbyists? Employers have also shown a desire to offer a premium for employers who can code and program.

Given this information, you may be thinking if programming is something that you can pursue. However, there are still several unanswered questions. When it comes to learning to program, how long will it take? What are the benefits of learning to code? We engaged experts from a range of fields to address your queries and provide their perspectives on the advantages of learning to program. We're happy to inform you why coding is a valuable talent worth bringing to your toolkit, whether you are a marketer, a mum, a company owner, or even just interested in the art.

Why develop coding skills?

Coding has a remarkable number of advantages. Here are a couple of the advantages of learning to code.

1. Jobs in programming have a high-income opportunity.

The income opportunities for computing and computer practitioners are one of the best and most visible attractions of writing code. But for a number of occupations, the Labor Statistics Bureau keeps track of wages and other relevant employment data.

Take a peek at the average annual wage data from the Bureau of Labor Statistics (BLS) for programming-related jobs in 2019:

- $73,760 for web developers

- $83,510 for computer systems and network administrators

- Computer programmers are paid $86,550 a year.

- Database operators are paid $93,750 a year.

- $107,510 for software engineers

To place that in context, in 2019, the national salary average for all jobs was $39,810.2. As you've seen, jobs that include any programming, scripting, or coding abilities pay more than the average.

2. The need for coding work is still high.

What use is a high wage if nobody is interested in hiring for the job? It seems that there is already plenty of scope in the field of coding.

The below are the latest BLS job development forecasts for the same programming and coding professions:

• Web developers account for 13% of the total.

• Administrators of computer systems and networks: 5%

• Computer program engineers (-7%).

• Database operators (9%).

• Software engineers make up 21% of the workforce.

As compared to the United States average of 5% rise, it's clear that a few occupations are outpacing the majority of others. Software programmers are an anomaly in this community, although others suggest that these predictions are affected by computer programming talents integrating into the other in-demand tech positions.

Although the job remains important, ever more hybrid roles are being integrated into the marketplace. As a trend, there are fewer work openings for "computer programmers" and more prospects that blend programming capabilities with other job names.

3. The capacity to code provides a fresh outlook on problem-solving.

"Learning to program has the unintended consequence of showing you how to analyze and think," tells Adrian Degus, CEO of Nuvro. He goes on to say that he used to be more open to emotionally fixing issues. His coding practice, on the other hand, has shown him how to solve challenges logically.

"Knowing reasoning at a profound level has exponentially strengthened my problem-solving ability," he continues.

In the simplest form, coding entails giving a machine a job to complete based on the conceptual rules you've developed. When you split down highly complicated functions, they become a series of smaller activities. This analytical and rational mindset to problem-solving could be useful for solving issues that aren't related to code.

Hilary Bird, a developer at CenturyLink, agrees, adding that learning to program has helped her in both her professional and personal life by helping her to step back and look at things from a different angle. She says, "I can split things down into tiny, independent pieces and find out how one affects the other." "This aids me in deciding which aspect of the issue to tackle first."

4. It allows you to have further job options.

It will help you expand your job opportunities and, in turn, render you a more adaptable applicant in a rapidly changing digital economy. Daniel Davidson, the founder of Dan Design., launched his work in digital printing but soon realized he was losing out on prospects due to the lack of coding skills.

"Coding has become the single most valuable skill I've acquired for my work career," Davidson notes. "I could be out of employment years earlier if I hadn't learned to code. It has been both liberating and profitable."

Even though your work doesn't enable you to have a profound knowledge of coding languages, Davidson says, it also helps because then you'll almost certainly be interacting with someone who does. Also as a hobby, coding will provide you with a basic comparison point and a greater comprehension of others that work in more complicated coding roles.

5. Learning to program could be a fun way for families to connect.

How much do you get the chance to teach your children something useful and new? Parents and their children have the opportunity to study the basics of computing and coding alongside.

Degus explains, "My 11-year-old daughter finally started to learn to program with me." "It was a difficult but satisfying experience. My daughter and I also chat about coding at the dining table, while the majority of the family mocks us for being nerds."

As the importance of coding grows, Christopher Prasad, manager at JooSMS, pointed out, engaging your children can be a perfect way to hold yourself responsible while still teaching them valuable skills.

"It's a great thing looking ahead and encouraging the youth of today," he says. "Educational institutions in the United Kingdom have already now taught programming to smaller kids because they understand what is necessary to create smartphones, apps, and more," he says.

Working with kid-friendly tools like Scratch, which introduces both you and your child to computing principles and systematic logic, is an excellent opportunity to explore the depths of writing code. When you progress to more specific languages and technologies, you will benefit from this foundational knowledge.

6. Coding may be helpful in unexpected places.

You may believe that coding skills are really only useful for people who work in highly skilled occupations. While it's clear that coding is more necessary for certain careers than others, it does not mean you cannot use coding skills in non-coding professions.

Mark Billion, a software architect and developer, claims that his coding skills have helped him in unlikely ways as a business specialist.

Billion explains, "We were allowed to use Python to write our ads algorithms, which spared us around $1,500 a month." "So, if you're in company business—coding is essential."

Billion's capacity to code helped him to optimize menial activities, saving him money in the process. That's a big bonus for small companies, which are mostly on a shoestring budget.

Learning the fundamentals of coding will render you a far more successful part of a team if you interact closely with developers and programmers.

Jake Lane, Press Cleaners' development manager, says, "While I'm mainly a marketer, possessing technological experience is one of the most valuable tools I can offer my team." "Being willing to make changes to the code base allows our developers to work on the most critical aspects of the project while still reducing production time."

You do not have to be a whiz at programming to profit from writing code. In certain market situations, knowing only enough to be beneficial is always a good advantage.

Chapter 1 - What is Python?

You cannot go wrong by learning CSS, HTML, and JavaScript if you choose to move to a job in web or app production (always a smart way to get into tech). However, if you really want to stick out in a packed field of candidates, you will need to introduce more languages to your knowledge base.

Since there are a lot of programming languages available today, this is where it can get complicated. How then can you tell the ones that are worthwhile to learn? T isn't about picking a chit out of a box— it's determining which coding language can provide you with the best payoff.

That takes us to the subject of studying Python.

1.1 An Overview

It is a general-purpose programming language, which implies that it may be used for various aspects of system and software creation, other than web development, unlike CSS, HTML, and JavaScript.

Python may be used for a variety of tasks, including:

• Handling large amounts of data and running statistical calculations

• Generating system scripts (directives that inform a computer what to do).

But don't be put off by Python's vast scope. Python, like the more commonly associated languages, is a simple-to-learn, high-demand coding language that will dramatically improve the odds of getting jobs and earning money.

1.2 For whom python is appropriate?

Python is indeed an emerging sensation in the coding community for two main reasons: it can do a wide variety of tasks and it is also a really beginner-friendly code. Python uses English keywords in its code syntax, making it simple to grasp and learn. Consider the following code, which will be used to display the message "Hello World" onto your computer using the Java language:

```
class helloworld {
    public static void main(String[] args) {
        System.out.println("Hello World!");
    }
}
```

For this basic function, that was a load of coding.

Have a peek at the following Python code for the same task:

```
print("Hello, World!")
```

Isn't it obvious which one you would like to deal with? Despite the fact that Python's syntax appears to be clear, it's used for tasks as complex as machine learning and artificial intelligence. Python is also ideal for a broad variety of people, such as:

- Beginner coders

- Software engineers

- Mobile and web app developers

- Data Scientists

- Along with anyone working around computer programming!

1.3 Why should you learn Python?

1. There are many python jobs available.

Indeed.com has over 69,000 Python-connected work vacancies as of this date. Python jobs with any degree of expertise and career interest exist, from quality engineer positions, entrance software engineer vacancies, and high-skilled jobs including artificial intelligence and machine learning engineers, Python coding may be used in a multitude of forms.

2. Python can get you an amazing salary.

Did we add that Python would pay you? Here are some of the mean wages by position, according to Indeed:

- $52,591 for a beginner software developer

- Engineer of quality Assurance: $61,460

- $80,984 for a Junior Python programmer

- $117,832 for a Senior Python programmer

- $142,029 for Machine Learning Engineers

We all should be studying Python right now, given wages like that (notably that $81k for junior Python programmers).

3. Python is super popular

Is the popularity of a computer language important? It does in certain ways. If the strongest programming language has no clients, it's like the proverbial tree falling in the woods- it does not matter when no one is using it. So the last move you need to do is waste time and resources researching a language that's not regularly used enough to give you a career.

According to The Economist, Python has been well on its way to become the world's highest-grossing programming language as of the last few years. Languages such as Lisp and FORTRAN have seen a dramatic drop in popularity, whereas languages such as C++ have remained stable yet flat. Languages such as JavaScript and Python, on the other hand, saw a sharp rise in popularity.

4. Learning python doesn't take long.

You may assume that learning Python takes years because it is such a strong and flexible language. Not at all! Python basics (stuff like Python's grammar, commands, and different data types), as per industry experts, can be mastered in as few as 7-9 weeks if you already have prior coding knowledge.

5. Python is a favorite of startups.

To prosper, startups must operate lean, which ensures that their digital goods (whether blogs, smartphone applications, or software programs) must be delivered within budget and on time. Python is a common language throughout the startup community due to its potential to help achieve any of these objectives.

Python's reliability and simplicity of use result in less development effort and time, a more efficient QA and debugging operation, and a higher average rate of return than more difficult-to-use coding options. Startups are an excellent way to land your first work and begin gathering business exposure, and learning Python would make you an even more appealing recruit.

6. The user community for python is really supportive.

Python is a programming language that is open source, which means that it is free to access and that anybody may change or build extensions for it. Since it is open-source, it can provide modules, plugins, and other resources that help it stay popular and efficient over time. However, open-source will only achieve its full capacity if there is a welcoming group of consumers who are invested in the language.

There is a community page on the website of python software foundation that links to many community forums in which you can meet other Python lovers for guidance, mentorship, motivation, or just to talk about Python's brilliance. So, what exactly are you checking for? There's space on the Python train for one more!

7. Python can help in both front and back end projects by working better together

You can earn a profit as a front-end developer, there is much more to it than that. Web servers and databases drive the back end (the hidden portions of webpages and mobile applications).

The Python Foundation speaks of utilizing Python as an "adhesive language" for sites and smartphone applications, they're referring to utilizing it to code back-end activities, enabling the virtual product's back and front ends to function together. Python is a great place to start if you want to incorporate back end or server-side skills to the front end arsenal (and also get nearer to having a complete full-stack development skillset).

8. Python is a versatile language

Since Python is a general-purpose language, it could do a lot, and that is why big tech companies like Facebook, Google, and

Instagram are using it. However, Python programming can also be used to create simple programs such as computer magic 8-ball and dice rolling simulations

Python's simplicity ensures that as a programmer, you will have a plethora of job opportunities. Python coding knowledge is an ability that allows you to work with a tech giant, create your own small-scale software projects, or work as a web developer, among other things.

9. Python does all the boring work for you.

Handling all those tedious, time-consuming software functions is one of the most difficult aspects of coding in tech. Copying data, moving and renaming directories, and transferring properties to repositories all sum up to a significant amount of downtime in the longer run.

Another environment where learning Python pays off is automation. Since Python allows you to write machine scripts, you can use it to build easy Python programs to automate repetitive jobs that chew up your time. Fully understanding how to simplify tasks with Python will save you a lot of time, which is a big selling point for studying the language.

10. Python can be used differently

Other languages render programming cumbersome and unwieldy... just not Python!

Python comes with a solid basic library (without other add-ons or frameworks) straight out of the package, allowing for faster coding. Pre-packaged "modules" are often included in the standard library of python, allowing developers to save time and make their scripts more uniformly organized by skipping the step of coding certain functions individually.

Then there is the idea that Python programming was designed with readability in mind because the language emphasizes English phrases rather than signs and punctuation. As a creator, this makes it easy to search code and manage and upgrade applications, websites, and smartphone apps.

11. It has add-ons for various tasks

No trouble if you need anything more flexible than the ready-to-use Python configuration. Python, including languages such as JavaScript, has a plethora of modules and plugins to meet the unique software requirements.

Python frameworks such as Django are built to render Python more powerful at developing web apps, whereas PyQt is a platform that enables Python to create Graphical User Interface (GUIs)—they handle user commands using on-screen graphics.

12. Python provides you with the ability to succeed anywhere in the tech world.

Learning Python coding would train you for much more than just web creation in the future—it will train you for the world of technological jobs in general.

What is the reason for this? Python language is used for a lot more than just standard programming. Python is, in particular, a leading language for evolving data fields such as:

- Artificial Intelligence

- Data Analysis

- Machine Learning

Chapter 2- How Python Works?

Python is one of the leading languages in programming. Here is a little overview of its working.

2.1 Easy to read and write

The way Python implements the utilization of indentation for comprehensibility is one of its most prominent features. Your code would not work if it is not properly indented. Every code block in Python must be indented to a similar degree. Here's an indication of this. Don't panic if you can't comprehend the code yet:

```python
def bigger_than_five(x):
  # The contents of a function are indented
  if x > 5:
    # This is another, even more indented block of code
    print("X is bigger than five")
  else:
    # And one more!
    print("x is 5 or smaller")
```

Since indentation is necessary, unlike Java, and C, Python doesn't require accolades to group code blocks. While it is a personal preference, most people believe that it helps Python to be simpler to read.

2.2 Compiled vs Interpreted

Python is an interpreted language.

When you execute a code in Python, the Python interpreter interprets the program on the fly. This is valid for CPython, the Python's reference implementation. Since Python is an interpreted coding language, it opens a file and begins interpreting it line by line, doing the necessary acts for each code. As the Python interpreter comes across print ("Hello") in your program, it will pass the specified string and print the message to your computer.

Languages that are compiled

Compared to compiled languages such as C, this is a very different technique. C's program is converted to low-level machine language, which can then be executed directly by the processor of the computer. Compiled coding is faster than interpreted code since there is no intermediary in interpreted code.

Benefits of interpreted code

When opposed to compilation ahead of time, an interpreted code has many advantages:

- You can use a text editor to write the code and then run it. There are no additional measures, such as compilation or connecting, required.

- You may simply just open a file and check the contents since it's plain text. Compiled coding, on the other hand, is not understandable by humans.

- It is independent to platform. Your program can run on every computer which has an interpreter for python. Compiled code is tied to a particular computer, such as Windows or Ubuntu, as well as a particular processing architecture, such as Intel.

Any of these benefits may also be a drawback. Interpreted languages, as previously said, are not powerful languages. Often, for vendors who wish to defend their copyright, the reality that the source code is simple to interpret and change is a disadvantage.

Between compiled and interpreted

A just-in-time compiler is a middle ground alternative (JIT). Your program is compiled when the software is running with JIT. JIT aims to balance the pace benefit of compiling ahead of time with the ease of interpretation. One of the biggest advantages of JIT is that one can optimize the code even when it's operating. Your code can get more optimized as it runs longer.

JIT compilation is well-known in the Java platform, but there is also PyPy, a JIT Python implementation. In certain ways, this project has progressed to the point that it can be used as a drop-in substitution.

2.3 Typed dynamically

Another benefit of interpreted code is that they make interactive typing possible. What exactly does it imply? I'll show you how with some basic JavaScript.

Here are few examples of Java variable declarations:

```java
String myName = "Erik";
int myAge = 37;
float mySalary = 1250.70;
```

You must define the exact form of each variable in a strongly typed coding language, such as String, float, etc. If objects are included, it becomes much more annoying.

We can do the same thing in Python without using types:

```python
my_name = "Erik"
my_age = 37
my_salary = 1250.70
```

As you see, the Python version is even more aesthetically pleasing!

Python dynamically determines the form of our variables when we execute this script. Let's say I want to find my annual profits by multiplying my income by 12, I'd have to take the following steps:

my income = 12 * my salary

Python will examine my salary, determine that it is a float-point number, and then execute the calculations. Python would not have complained if my salary had been a string. When it detects a string, it simply creates a new one of 12 repeats of the string! In such instances, Java, on the other hand, will throw an error.

There are several benefits of dynamic typing. It allows it easy to get started easily in general. Some would argue that it is more vulnerable to errors. If a type error occurs in a strong typed coding language like Java, the code may not compile. Python would most likely continue to run, although the result will be alarming. My experience has been that it does not really happen too much, and that you will notice it while testing and simply fix the issue.

2.4 Garbage collection

Variables are a concept in Python. Any value, such as a string of text or a number may be stored in a variable.

Every variable declared consumes memory on your device. This can easily add up, particularly if you're writing long-running projects. But you'll need a way to get rid of variables you're no longer using.

In certain languages, this cleanup must be done directly. A memory leak is a form of error that may occur as a result of this. If you produce a little error and fail to clean up, the application can gradually use all usable memory. Fortunately for us, Python's garbage collector automatically removes unused variables!

I won't go through the boring specifics here but feel sure that Python can do an excellent job and could never remove a variable that is in need.

2.5 Python 2 and Python 3

Python 3 and 2 have been built and preserved along with each other for a long time. The main explanation for this is that Python 3 programming is not fully backward compatible with that of Python 2. This incompatibility resulted in a slower pace of acceptance. Many users were content with version 2 and saw little need to update. Furthermore, Python 3 was slow than Python 2 at first. Python 3 began to gain popularity as it continued to improve and gain new capabilities.

Since Python 3 has become the standard and only supported edition, this book focuses solely on it. Python 2 code can be encountered in the modern world.

2.6 Learning the basics

You ought to be able to get a decent start even though you have no previous programming experience. We'll take things slowly at first, and before you realize, you'll have a strong foundation in:

- Strings

- Numbers

- Dictionaries

- Variables

- Booleans

- Iterators

- Loops

- And a lot more!

This book to Python won't go into the nitty-gritty of these topics, but rather will skim the rim and expose you to the fundamental concepts.

2.7 Downloading Python

You'll need Python installed on your device before you begin.

Type python in a command-line interface to see whether you have an updated version of Python enabled. As a Python interpreter responds, it may have a version code in its view. Python ensures every effort to ensure backward compatibility across major Python releases, so every Python 3.x update can suffice. Python 3.x and Python 2.x are not completely compliant by design. If python launches a Python 2.x code interpreter, type python3 to see if a more recent version is already available.

For Windows, use py initially - this is the comparatively new Python Launcher, that has a greater probability of preventing path problems that can arise when programs aren't installed into the limited collection of popular locations that are checked by default on Windows. With a single button, the Python installer will pick all of the different variants you've loaded.

You should download the latest stable version of Python. It is the one with the most downloads and isn't a beta or alpha version. The most recent versions of Python can be found on the Python downloads website. They can be downloaded from the page's yellow download keys.

Microsoft® Windows®

The Python for Windows website has the most up-to-date Windows versions. You may choose between 32-bit (marked x86) and 64-bit (marked x86-64) models of Windows, as well as many installer flavors for both. The Python foundation team believes that there should be a standard that you should not have to worry about, so the "x86 executable installer" option is available when you click the yellow-colored download option on the primary download page. This is really a good option: even though you have 64-bit Windows, you wouldn't need the 64-bit Python; the 32-bit Python would suffice.

Mac

Look at Python of Mac OS X site. MacOS provides a framework build of Python 2. But, you cannot use this for the coding asks; instead, install a new Python 3.x edition. After (Catalina) 10.5, there would be no default framework Python.

Linux

Setup the python3 along with python3-devel packs on CentOS, Red Hat, or Fedora.

Install the python3.x along with python3.x-dev files for Ubuntu or Debian.

Chapter 3- Basic Rules and Practical Applications

You should be having an installed Python 3 interpreter on hand, at this stage. If you still haven't and need help to set up python correctly, then please look at the previous chapter.

This is what you will be learning in this chapter: Now that you possess an installed Python setup, you will observe how to write Python code lines and run some Python programs. At the end of the chapter, you will have learned how to:

- Execute the code in a script file using the command line

- Operate Python interactively and efficiently by writing code directly in the interpreter.

- You will learn about some basic **string**, Boolean and numeric types that are Python's built-in data types. You will understand what objects of such types look like, and how to use and represent them.

- Work in an (IDE) Integrated Development Environment of Python.

- You will also get an idea of built-in **functions of Python.** These are pre-typed code blocks that you can make good use of. We will start with the print () function.

Let's start writing Python programs!

3.1 Interaction with Python

Hello, World!

It is an old tradition in the world of computers and programming that the very first code line typed in a freshly downloaded language is a small program that displays the simple string Hello, World! On the screen.

Note: It is a time-honored custom that started in the 70s.

Displaying something on the screen is also referred to as printing

The easiest Python 3 code line to print Hello, World! is:

Print ("Hello, World!")

We will learn some different ways for executing this code later.

Interacting with the interpreter

The simplest way to begin talking with Python is by using a REPL (Read-Eval-Print Loop) environment. This simply means opening the interpreter and writing commands to it in a direct manner. The interpreter will:

- **R**ead the code you write

- **E**valuate and execute the code

- **P**rint the result (if there is any) to the screen

- **L**oopback and repeat the process again

The program continues to run in this way until you tell the interpreter to stop. Most of the code examples in this chapter are shown as a REPL interaction.

Opening the Interpreter

In a GUI environment, such as Windows, it is probable that the installing process puts an icon sign on your desktop which starts Python.

For instance, in Windows, there should be a program group located in **Start** named **Python 3.x**, and below it, a menu element named **Python 3.x (64 or 32-bit).**

Clicking on this open the Python interpreter:

Other than this, you may start a terminal window and get the interpreter using the command line. How you go about to open a terminal window may vary based on which OS (operating system) you are using:

- In Linux or MacOS, it is called **Terminal**.

- In Windows, it's called the **Command Prompt**.

Using your OS's searching function to look for "terminal" in the MacOS or "command" in the Windows should locate it.

Once the terminal window is opened, simply just type python. After that, you will see a reaction from the interpreter.

The below example is taken from the window of Command Prompt of Windows:

```
Windows Console

C:\Users\john>python
Python 3.6.0 (v3.6.0:41df79263a11, Dec 23 2016, 07:18:10) [MSC v.1900 32 bit (Intel)]
Type "help", "copyright", "credits" or "license" for more information.
>>>
```

Technical Note: If you are using Linux and if it has both Python 2 and 3 installed then simply typing Python will open Python 2. To start Python 3; simply type python3. Or if you have different versions of Python then be more specific. For example, type python3.6.

If there is no >>> prompt, then that means you're not speaking with the Python interpreter. This may be because Python isn't installed or maybe it is not in the session's path of your terminal windows. It is also likely that you have not found the right command to run it.

Executing the Code

If the prompt, is visible, you are successful! The next stage is to execute the code that prints Hello, World! on the screen:

1. Make sure that the >>> prompt is shown, and the cursor is located after it.

2. Write the command line exactly as shown below.

3. Press Enter on your keyboard.

The Python interpreter's result should be shown on the line after. You can identify that it is the output as there is no >>> prompt.

```
Python                                                          >>>

>>> print("Hello, World!")
Hello, World!
```

If your screen looks like the image above, then you have successfully executed your very first Python console code! Congratulations!

Did you not get the same result? Maybe you made one of the following errors:

- You didn't enclose "hello world" in quotes.

- You wrote different types of quotes at the beginning and end.

- You missed the parentheses.

- Maybe you entered extra spaces before the command

If you got any type of error message, then go back and make that you wrote the code exactly the same as the image above.

Closing the Python Interpreter

When you're done using the interpreter, you may quit the REPL session in one of several methods:

- Write exit () and then press Enter.

- In Windows, press the Ctrl+Z and then press Enter.

- In MacOS or Linux, press Ctrl+D. The interpreter will terminate immediately without needing to press enter.

- If you are unable to do these, you can just close the window of the interpreter. This is not the ideal way, but it will do the job. It is "unprogrammer like" to do this.

3.2 Running a Script Using Command Line

Typing commands in the interpreter is good for quick tests and exploring functions and features.

But eventually, as you make more complex programs, you will write longer code that you'll have to run and edit repeatedly. You obviously do not want to type the code repeatedly in the interpreter. To go around this, you will have to make a script file.

A script in Python is a set of code that can be reused. It is basically a Python program—a sequenced set of Python commands—contained inside a file. The program can be run by stating the script file to the Python interpreter.

Scripts in Python are just plain text, so they can be edited using any text editor. The following editors below are usually pre-installed with their operating systems:

- Unix/Linux: vi or vim

- Windows: Notepad

- MacOS: TextEdit

Using whichever text editor you have selected, make a script file named hello.py and type the hello word code shown previously in an image.

Then save that file, and keep track of the folder or directory that you chose to save your file in.

Open a terminal or command prompt window. If the working directory is the same as the save location of your file, you may simply state the name of the file as an argument of command-line in the interpreter as:

```
python hello.py
```

For instance, it will look like this in Windows:

```
C:\Users\john\Documents\test>dir
 Volume in drive C is JFS
 Volume Serial Number is 1431-F891

 Directory of C:\Users\john\Documents\test

05/20/2018  01:31 PM    <DIR>          .
05/20/2018  01:31 PM    <DIR>          ..
05/20/2018  01:31 PM                24 hello.py
               1 File(s)             24 bytes
               2 Dir(s)  92,557,885,440 bytes free

C:\Users\john\Documents\test>python hello.py
Hello, World!
```

If the script isn't in the working directory, then you run it using a different method. You will just have to state the exact path to it:

```
C:\>cd
C:\

C:\>python c:\Users\john\Documents\test\hello.py
Hello, World!
```

In MacOS or Linux, it should appear more like this:

```
jfs@jfs-xps:~$ pwd
/home/jfs

jfs@jfs-xps:~$ ls
hello.py

jfs@jfs-xps:~$ python hello.py
Hello, World!
```

A .py extension required in a script file. The interpreter will successfully run the file irrespective of the files name, as long as the file name is properly specified on the command line:

```
Shell

jfs@jfs-xps:~$ ls
hello.foo

jfs@jfs-xps:~$ cat hello.foo
print("Hello, World!")

jfs@jfs-xps:~$ python hello.foo
Hello, World!
```

But providing the Python files with a .py extension is very useful as it makes them easier to identify. In MacOS and Windows, this will even allow for setting useful file associations. If this is done then clicking on the file will simply run the program.

3.3 Data types

Now that we have learned how to use the Python interpreter and run Python commands. It is time to venture into the world of Python. We will start by discussing the built-in basic data types of Python.

Integers

In Python 3, there isn't any limit to how long your integer value can be. But obviously, it is limited by the memory that your system possesses, basically, all things are, but above than that, an integer may be as big as you desire it to be:

```
Python                                                                      >>>

>>> print(12312312312312312312312312312312312312312312312312312312312312 + 1)
123123123123123123123123123123123123123123123124
```

Python interprets a line of decimal digits without the need of the prefix to be a decimal value:

```
Python                                                                      >>>

>>> print(10)
10
```

Floating-Point values

The float type corresponds to a floating-point number in python. float values are shown with a point, such that is used with decimals. As another option, the character E or e followed by a negative or positive integer may be used to append to show scientific notation:

```
Python

>>> 4.2
4.2
>>> type(4.2)
<class 'float'>
>>> 4.
4.0
>>> .2
0.2

>>> .4e7
4000000.0
>>> type(.4e7)
<class 'float'>
>>> 4.2e-4
0.00042
```

Complex Numbers

Do you remember complex numbers from school? A+Bi? They can be used in Python. Such numbers are written as <real>+<imaginary>j. Look at the example below:

```
Python

>>> 2+3j
(2+3j)
>>> type(2+3j)
<class 'complex'>
```

Strings

Strings are sequenced data characters. Strings are called str in Python.

String characters may be specified using single or even double-quotes. All of the data characters between the opening quote and matching closing quote are a part of that string:

```
Python                                                                    >>>

>>> print("I am a string.")
I am a string.
>>> type("I am a string.")
<class 'str'>

>>> print('I am too.')
I am too.
>>> type('I am too.')
<class 'str'>
```

A string may have as many characters as you want in Python. The only limitation, as we said before, is the memory resources of your device. A string may also be empty.

What if you need to have a character quote as part of your string? Your first thought may be to do something similar to this:

```
Python                                                                    >>>

>>> print('This string contains a single quote (') character.')
SyntaxError: invalid syntax
```

If you try it, you will as above, that it does not work as well as you expected. The string in the example above starts using a single quote, so the Python interpreter thinks that the single quote that comes next, the quote in brackets which was put to be a part of

44

your string, is the quote that is used to close. The last single quote is, as a result, out of place and results in the syntax error above.

If you desire to add either of the quote characters inside the string, the easiest method is to enclose the string using the other type of quotation mark. If you want a string to have a double quote, enclose it with single quotation marks and vice versa:

```
Python                                                          >>>

>>> print("This string contains a single quote (') character.")
This string contains a single quote (') character.

>>> print('This string contains a double quote (") character.')
This string contains a double quote (") character.
```

Escaping Sequences in the String

Sometimes, you may want Python to execute a character sequence or a single character inside a string in a different manner. This can be done in two different ways:

- You might want to give special action to characters inside a string which normally would be not given.

- You might want to not give the special interpretation that some specified characters are given inside a string.

A backslash () character may be used to do this. In a string, a backslash character means that one or maybe more characters after it should be handled differently. (This is known as an escape sequence since the backslash allows the next character sequence to "escape" the original meaning.)

Let's take a look at how this happens.

Suppressing the Meaning of Special Characters

You've also seen the issues that may arise when attempting to use characters of the quote in a string. You can't define a single-quoted character inside a string enclosed using single quotes since the single-quoted character has a particular significance for that string—it has the function of terminating the string:>>>

```
Python                                                              >>>

>>> print('This string contains a single quote (') character.')
SyntaxError: invalid syntax
```

In a string, putting a backslash at the front of the quote symbol "escapes" it, causing Python to ignore its normal special purpose. It is then easily translated as a single quote individual:

>>>>>>>>

A single quote appears in this string.

The following even fits in a series separated by double quotes:

```
>>> print('This string contains a single quote (\') character.')
This string contains a single quote (') character.
```

The following even fits in a series separated by double quotes:

>>>

```
>>> print("This string contains a double quote (\") character.")
This string contains a double quote (") character.
```

The table below shows the escape sequences that allow Python to ignore the standard special meaning of characters inside a string:

Escape Character	How they are normally interpreted	Interpretation after "Escape"
\"	Stops string with a double quote enclosing	Literally types double quote (")
\'	Stops string with single quote enclosing	Literal literally types single quote (')
\\	Introduces the escape sequence	Literally types backslash (\)

\newline	Stops input line	The Newline is ignored

Usually, a newline addition stops the line input. So pushing Enter in between the string will make Python think that it's incomplete:

```
Python                                                        >>>

>>> print('a

SyntaxError: EOL while scanning string literal
```

Provide a backslash before every newline to split up a string across over than one line, the newlines will then be disregarded:

```
Python                                                        >>>

>>> print('a\
... b\
... c')
abc
```

A backlash escape can also be used to add a literal backslash inside the string:

```
Python                                                        >>>

>>> print('foo\\bar')
foo\bar
```

Characters with a Special Meaning

Let's pretend you need to make a string with a tab character inside it. You will be able to inject a tab character straight into the code in certain text editors. However, several programmers believe it is a bad practice for several purposes:

- You couldn't tell the difference between a series of spaces and tab characters but the system can. Space and tab characters are virtually invisible to a person reading the program.

- Certain REPL Python environments do not enable tabs to be inserted into code.

- Certain text editors are set up to automatically remove tab characters by extending them to the requisite amount of spaces.

An escape sequence \t: can be used to specify a tab character in Python (and now almost all other modern programming languages). >>>

```
Python                                                              >>>
>>> print('foo\tbar')
foo     bar
```

The \t escape sequence causes the t letter to give away its standard meaning, a literal t. In its place, the sequences are interpreted by Python as a tab character.

Here is a collection of escape sequences that allow Python to read in a specific way rather than literally:

The Escape Sequence	The "Escaped" Interpretation
\b	(BS) Backspace ASCII character
\a	(BEL) Bell ASCII character
\n	(LF) Linefeed ASCII character
\f	(FF) Formfeed ASCII character
\r	(CR) Carriage Return ASCII character
\uxxxx	16-bit hex value Unicode character xxxx
\N{<name>}	Unicode database Character with given <name>
\t	(TAB) Horizontal Tab ASCII character
\v	(VT) Vertical Tab ASCII character
\Uxxxxxxxx	32-bit hex value Unicode character xxxxxxxx
\xhh	Character with hexa value hh
\ooo	Character with octa value ooo

Example:

```
Python                                                            >>>
>>> print("a\tb")
a    b
>>> print("a\141\x61")
aaa
>>> print("a\nb")
a
b
>>> print('\u2192 \N{rightwards arrow}')
→ →
```

This kind of escape sequence is commonly used to add characters that are difficult to produce with the keyboard or that aren't easily recognizable or printable.

Raw strings

A raw string literal is followed by an R or r, which indicates that the corresponding string's escape sequences aren't translated. The backslash is not removed from

the string:

```
Python                                                  >>>

>>> print('foo\nbar')
foo
bar
>>> print(r'foo\nbar')
foo\nbar

>>> print('foo\\bar')
foo\bar
>>> print(R'foo\\bar')
foo\\bar
```

Triple-Quoted Strings

There is also another method of enclosing strings in the Python language. Strings that are triple quoted are enclosed by matching sequences of 3 double quotes or three single quotes. The Escape sequence still operates in triple-quoted string texts, but double quotes, newlines, and single quotes can be added without the need for escape. This gives an easy method to make a string with both double and single quotes inside it:

>>>

```
Python                                                  >>>

>>> print('''This string has a single (') and a double (") quote.''')
This string has a single (') and a double (") quote.
```

As newlines can be added without the need to escape them, multiple strings are allowed:

```
>>> print("""This is a
string that spans
across several lines""")
This is a
string that spans
across several lines
```

Boolean

Python 3 has a data type called Boolean. Items of Boolean data type can have

one of a possible of two values, False or True:

```
Python                                                          >>>
>>> type(True)
<class 'bool'>
>>> type(False)
<class 'bool'>
```

Expressions of Python are frequently evaluated in a Boolean form, which means they are perceived to reflect false or truth, as you'll see later in the book. A true value in Boolean is often referred to as "truthy," while one which is false is referred to as "falsy." (The word "falsy" is sometimes spelled "falsey.")

An object of Boolean type's "truthiness" is self-evident: Boolean objects equal to True are called truthy (true), whereas those equivalent to False are called falsy (false). Non-Boolean properties, on the other hand, maybe analyzed in a Boolean sense and judged to be false or true.

3.4 Built-in Functions

As of Python 3.6, the interpreter offers a total of 68 built-in functions. Many of these would be discussed in detail in the subsequent topics if they arise.

For the time being, a quick rundown is provided to offer you an idea of what's usable. Many of the explanations that follow apply to subjects and ideas that will be covered in upcoming lessons.

Math Functions

Function	Working
divmod()	Returns remainder and quotient of division
abs()	Returns the absolute value of the number
min()	Returns smallest argument from items inside an iterable

max()	Returns largest given argument from items inside an iterable
round()	Rounds floating-point values
pow()	Raises numbers to a specified power
sum()	Sums up the items inside an iterable

Type changing functions

Function	Working
bin()	Changes an integer to a string that is binary
ascii()	Produces a string having a representation of an item
bool()	Changes an argument to Boolean
complex()	Gives a complex number made from arguments
chr()	Returns the string representation of the character specified by the integer argument

float()	Returns floating-point objects made from a string or a number
int()	Produces an integer made from a string or a number
hex()	Changes an integer to hexadecimal string
ord()	Returns the integer representation of specified character
oct()	Changes an integer value to a string which is octal
repr()	Returns strings having a representation of an item
type()	Tells you the type of the object stated or makes an entirely new type object
str()	Returns string versions of objects

Iterators and Iterables

Function	Working
any()	Returns value True if any of the elements in an iterable are true
all()	Returns value True if all of the elements in an iterable are true
enumerate()	Produces a tuples list having values and indices from an iterable
iter()	Produces an iterator object
sorted()	Produces a sorted list of an iterable
len()	Tells the length of specified object
next()	Gets the next item from specified iterator
map()	Applies specified function to every single item of iterables
range()	Presents a range of integers
slice()	Produces a slice object
reversed()	Returns a reverse iterator
filter()	Filters the elements in an iterable

Function	Working
zip()	Makes an iterator that totals elements in iterables

Composite Data Types

Function	Working
bytes()	Makes and returns a byte object (much like bytearray, but irreversible)
bytearray()	Makes and returns objects of bytearray class
frozenset()	Creates an object which is a frozenset
dict()	Creates an object which is of dict type
object()	Creates a new object which is featureless
list()	Creates an object of list type
tuple()	Creates an object of tuple type
set()	Creates an object of set type

Classes, Inheritance, and attributes

Function	Working
delattr()	Deletes an attribute of an object
classmeth od()	Will return class method of a function
hasattr()	Will return True if the object has the stated attribute
getattr()	Returns value of a stated object attribute
property()	Returns property value of a class
setattr()	Sets value of named object attribute
issubclass()	Tells if a class is a subclass of a specified class
isinstance( )	Tells if an object is of a specified class instance
super()	Returns proxy objects that delegate method callings to a sibling or parent class

Input and Output

Function	Working
input()	Reads the input from console
format()	Changes a value to a representation that is formatted
print()	Prints in console or a text stream
open()	Opens specified file and then returns an object from the file

Variables, Scope, and References

Function	Working
globals()	Will return a dictionary that represents the current symbol global table
dir()	Returns list of names in a list of object attributes or a current local scope

vars()	Returns the __dict__ attribute of a module, object, or class
locals( )	Updates and then returns dictionary which represents the current symbol local table
id()	Returns identity of object

Miscellaneous

Function	Working
compile()	Compiles the source into AST object or a code
callable()	Returns value True if the object is callable
exec()	Does dynamic execution of the code
eval()	Evaluates an expression of Python
memoryview( )	Gives a memory view of an object
help()	Starts the help system
__import__()	Invoke byimport statement

staticmethod( )	Returns static method of a function
hash()	Returns hash value of object

You studied Python's built-in data forms and functions in this lesson.

So far, all of the references have just distorted and shown constant values. In almost all applications, you'll want to generate objects that shift in value when the software runs.

3.5 Basic operators

So, Python is a fantastic mathematician. In reality, it can easily take the place of your calculator. A confession: I constantly use the REPL of Python as a calculator!

We have learned to use the plus sign (+). It's the same as normal algebra. Let's take a look at a few of the operations available. Feel free to experiment with this:

Operation	Label	Working
+	Addition Symbol	2 +3 == 5
−	Subtraction Symbol	7 – 5 == 2
*	Multiplication Symbol	5 * 4 == 20
/	Division Symbol	7 / 2 == 3.5

Most of you must know these basic operators.

Here is something a little different:

Operation	Name	Working
%	Modulus Symbol	10 % 2 == 2
//	Floor division Symbol	11 // 2 == 5
**	Exponential Symbol	2 ** 4 == 16

Operator precedence

It is the order using which Python works out the numbers and the operators, it is very similar to math. For instance, division and multiplication come before subtraction and addition. If you are confused, you can use brackets, or just simply try it using the REPL.

Let us look at some examples:

```
>>> 2 + 4 * 3
14
```

```
>>> (2 + 4) * 3
18
```

```
>>> 1 + 2 ** 2
5
```

```
>>> 1 / 2 * 8
4.0
```

Chapter 4- Making Your Own Program

We have already learned about printing in the previous chapters. Functions and data types were also discussed. Now going forward:

4.1 Declaring Types of Variable Strings

What is a Variable?

A variable in python is a memory location reserved for storing values. A Python variable code, in other terms, provides data to the machine for processing.

Variable Types in Python

In Python, each value has a datatype. Numbers, Lists, Tuple, String, Dictionaries, and other data types exist in Python. Variables in Python can be named anything, including alphabet letters like a, ac, acc, and so on.

Declaring and using a Variable

Let's look at an example. We will be defining a variable and name it "a" and then print it.

```
a=100
print (a)
```

You can also re-declare a variable that has already been declared, this will change its value:

```python
# Declare a variable and initialize it
f = 0
print(f)
# re-declaring the variable works
f = 'guru99'
print(f)
```

Concatenation of strings

Let's see how you may concatenate various data types such as string and numbers. We'll concatenate "Guru" and"99," for example.

Unlike Java, which concatenates numbers with strings without declaring the numbers as strings, in Python, declaring variables necessitates declaring the numbers as strings, or else a TypeError may occur.

The below codes output will be undefined:

```python
a="Guru"
b = 99
print a+b
```

The integer needs to be declared as string. Python only concatenates data of the same type. We have done this using the built-in function discussed in the previous chapter:

```
a="Guru"
b = 99
print(a+str(b))
```

Local and global variable in Python

In Python, there are two kinds of variables: local and global variables. When declaring a variable in Python, you define it as a variable that is global, if you wish to use that in your application or module, and as a variable that is local, if you only want to use it in one method or function.

Let's look at the distinction between global and local variables in Python variable forms in the code below.

Let's describe a Python variable, in which the variable "f" has a global scale and is given the number 101, which would be printed in the output.

Variable f is defined in the function once more and has a local reach. The value is assigned to it, and it is printed as an output. This Python declaration variable is distinct from the previously established global variable "f."

If the local variable is deleted until the function call is completed. As we print "f" at line 12, it shows the value f=101 of the global variable.

```
1    # Declare a variable and initialize it
2    f = 101  ①
3    print(f)
4
5    # Global vs. local variables in functions
6    def someFunction():
7    # global f
8        f = 'I am learning Python'  ②
9        print(f)
10
11   someFunction()
12   print(f)  ③
13
```

> **f is a local variable declared inside the function.**

Run Python5.2

```
"C:\Users\DK\Desktop\Python code\Python Test\Python 5\PythonCode.
5/PythonCode5/Python5.2.py"
101  ①
I am learning Python  ②
101  ③
```

```
# Declare a variable and initialize it
f = 101
print(f)
# Global vs. local variables in functions
def someFunction():
# global f
    f = 'I am learning Python'
    print(f)
someFunction()
print(f)
```

May reference the variable globally in a function, with the Python variable declaration by using the term; **global.**

1. The variable "f" has a **global** scope and is given a value of 101 that is printed in the output.

2. The variable f is set by using the term **global.** This isn't **local**, but the very same global variable we declared earlier. So, when the value is printed, the output result is 101.

3. We altered the "f" value in the function. When the call function is done with, the value of the variable that we changed "f" remains. On line 12, when the value of "f" is printed again, it shows "changing global variable".

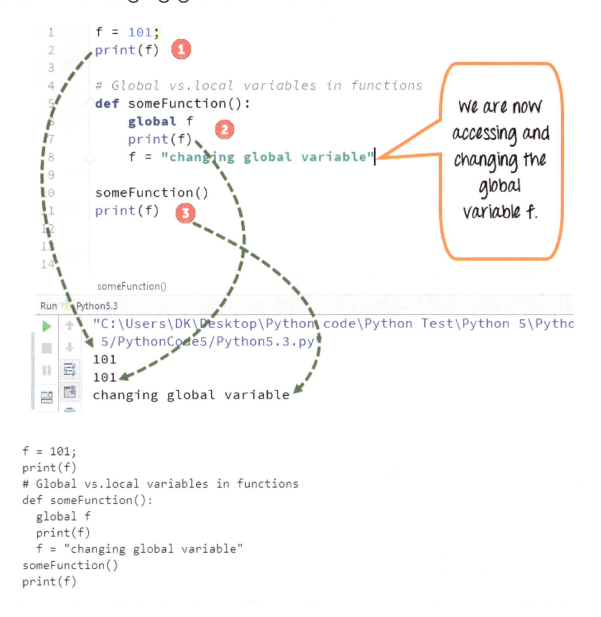

```
f = 101;
print(f)
# Global vs.local variables in functions
def someFunction():
  global f
  print(f)
  f = "changing global variable"
someFunction()
print(f)
```

Deleting a variable

Variables in Python are deleted using the "del" command. After which the variable is completely removed from the program.

```
f = 11;
print(f)
del f
print(f)
```

The output of this code will be a name error as f is no longer defined.

Variables Summary

- Variables are "envelopes" or "buckets" in which knowledge can be stored and retrieved. Python, like every other computer language, stores knowledge in variables.

- Variables can be named for every letter of the alphabet, such as a, AA, abc, and so on.

- And after you've declared variables already, you may re-declare them.

- You can't just concatenate numbers and string in Python; you have to designate them as separate variables first, and then you may concatenate string and number.

- Constants in Python are categories of variables that have a fixed value that can't be modified. Constants in Python are usually referenced from different files.

- Variable types in Python: Global and local

- When you wish to include a local variable in the current function, declare it.

- When you choose to use the same variable in the entire code then, declare a global variable.

- The keyword "del" is used to remove a variable.

4.2 Python Tuples

In the Python language, there are four different forms of collection data:

1. A **list** is an orderly and changeable set of items. Allows for the development of duplicate participants.

2. **Tuple** is an unchangeable and ordered set. Allows for the existence of duplicate members.

3. A **set** is an unsorted and unindexed array. There are no duplicate participants.

4. A **dictionary** is a changeable and ordered* list. There are no duplicate participants.

Dictionaries are now ordered as of Python 3.7. Dictionaries before Python 3.6 are not ordered.

Tuple Matching

Tuple matching is a way of grouping tuples in Python by comparing the 2nd element in each tuple. In Python language, it is accomplished using a dictionary and testing the second variable in each tuple. We may create new tuples by combining parts of established tuples.

Tuples are written using round brackets in Python, with the following syntax:

Tup = ('march','april','may')

An empty tuple can be written using brackets that show nothing:

tup = ();

Even if there is only one value, a comma is needed when composing a tuple for an individual value. You must also add a semicolon at the end, as seen below.

Tup = (60,);

Assignment of tuples

The tuple assignment function in Python allows you to delegate several variables at once. We've allocated tuple 1 to the person's details, such as name, title, year of birth, and so forth, and tuple 2 to the values, such as numbers (1,2....,7).

As an example,

(Name, title, year of birth, favorite film and year, career, place of birth) = Robert

The code is as follows:

```
tup1 = ('Robert', 'Carlos','1965','Terminator 1995', 'Actor','Florida');
tup2 = (1,2,3,4,5,6,7);
print(tup1[0])
print(tup2[1:4])
```

Tuple 1 contains a list of Robert's information, while Tuple 2 contains a list of numbers. The value for [0] is called in the tuple and for tuple 2, the value between 1 and 4 is called.

Execute the code- It provides the name Robert for the 1st tuple while for the 2nd tuple it returns numbers (2, 3, 4).

Packing and unpacking are also terms. Packing is when a value is placed into a new tuple and unpacking is when we extract the values back into their variables. Here is a short example:

```
x = ("Guru99", 20, "Education")    # tuple packing
(company, emp, profile) = x    # tuple unpacking
print(company)
print(emp)
print(profile)
```

Comparison of Tuples

Tuples can be compared with a comparison operator.

Each tuple's first element is used to begin the comparison. If they don't match =, or >, it moves on to the next part, and so on.

It all begins with a comparison of the first aspect of each tuple.

Let's take a look at an example.

#case 1

```
a=(5,6)
b=(1,4)
if (a>b):print("a is bigger")
else: print("b is bigger")
```

#case 2

```
a=(5,6)
b=(5,4)
if (a>b):print("a is bigger")
else: print ("b is bigger")
```

#case 3

```
a=(5,6)
b=(6,4)
if (a>b):print("a is bigger")
else: print("b is bigger")
```

Case 1: Each tuple's comparison begins with the first element. Since 5>1 in this scenario, the output is larger.

Case 2: Each tuple's comparison begins with the first part. In this scenario, 5>5 is an inconclusive result. As a result, it moves on to the next part. As 6>4, the output is larger.

Case 3: Each tuple's comparison begins with the first part. In this scenario, 5>6 is untrue. As a result, it enters the else block and outputs "b is larger."

Using tuples as dictionary keys

We need to use tuples as keys if we need to construct a composite key for use in

a dictionary because a tuple is hashable and lists are not.

For example, if we choose to construct a telephone directory that maps initial-name, last-name, phone numbers, and so on, we'll need to use a composite key. Considering that the variables were declared as first and last numbers, we may compose the following dictionary assignment statement:

```
directory[last,first] = number
```

The term is a tuple within the parentheses. To access this dictionary, we might use tuple assignment inside a for loop.

```
for last, first in directory:


    print first, last, directory[last, first]
```

We will discuss loops and iterators in detail in the coming topics.

Dictionaries can return the tuples list by calling the items, where every tuple is a value key pair.

```
a = {'x':100, 'y':200}
b = list(a.items())
print(b)
```

Tuples can't be deleted since they're immutable. Tuple items can't be deleted or removed from. However, the keyword "del" may be used to fully delete a tuple.

Slicing

We use a special feature named slicing to get specific sets of elements from a list or tuple. Slicing isn't just for tuples; it's even for arrays and lists.

```
x = ("a", "b","c", "d", "e")
print(x[2:4])
```

This code will give the output (''c,'d').

Multiple different tasks can be performed using the built-in functions we discussed in the previous chapter. They can be really useful once mastered.

4.3 Python Dictionaries

In Python, a dictionary is an unordered, changeable collection of data that stores key-value pairs. The dictionary's key-value pairs map the key to its corresponding value, rendering it more efficient. Curly brackets ({}) are used to enclose comma-separated lists of key-value pairs when declaring a python dictionary. Values and keys are the 2 parts of the Python Dictionary. Values may be within a list or a list while keys must be single elements.

This is the basic syntax

Dict = { ' Tim': 18, xyz,.. }

Dictionaries are listed in curly braces, in these curly braces, values and keys are declared. Keys are separated from their values by a colon (:), and commas separate the elements.

Key properties

When using dictionary keys, there are several things to keep in mind.

There can't be greater than one entrance per key (duplicate keys aren't allowed)

The dictionary's values can be of any kind, but the key has to be immutable, such as numbers, strings, and tuples.

In dictionaries of Python, keys are case sensitive, so the same key name for different cases is considered as a different setting. Look at this example code:

```python
Dict = {'Tim': 18,'Charlie':12,'Tiffany':22,'Robert':25}
print((Dict['Tiffany']))
```

In this code, there is a dictionary named "Dict". The age and name of the man is declared in the dictionary, where the key is the name, the value is the age. Running the code will return you the age of Tiffany.

Copying in Dictionary

You can copy an entire dictionary into a second dictionary. For example:

```python
Dict = {'Tim': 18,'Charlie':12,'Tiffany':22,'Robert':25}
Boys = {'Tim': 18,'Charlie':12,'Robert':25}
Girls = {'Tiffany':22}
studentX=Boys.copy()
studentY=Girls.copy()
print(studentX)
print(studentY)
```

We have the initial dictionary (Dict) having the names and ages of boys and girls combined, but we want the boys and girls lists to be different, so we created another dictionary with the names "Girls" and "boys".

We've produced two separate dictionaries, "student Y" and "student X," in which all of the values and values and keys from the girl dictionary are copied to student X, and the Boys are copied into student Y.

And now you will not have to look at the whole collection in the key dictionary (Dict) to figure out who is a girl and who is a boy; all you have to do is print student X for boys and Student Y for girls.

As a result, when you execute the student Y and student X dictionaries, they can show all of the elements included in the "girls" and "boys" dictionaries separately.

Updating Dictionaries

You may also update dictionaries by bringing a new key-value pair or an entry to an entry that already exists or by deleting an entry. In the example below, we will attach "Sarah" to our dictionary.

```
Dict = {'Tim': 18,'Charlie':12,'Tiffany':22,'Robert':25}
Dict.update({"Sarah":9})
print(Dict)
```

We make use of the function Dict.update to bring Sarah to our dictionary. Running the code will print the dictionary with Sarah in it.

You may remove any item from the dictionary. If you do not want Charlie inside the list, use the below code to delete the key element.

```
Dict = {'Tim': 18,'Charlie':12,'Tiffany':22,'Robert':25}
del Dict ['Charlie']
print(Dict)
```

Running this code will print the dictionary without Charlie. The del method is used for deleting.

Checking if a key exists inside a dictionary

For a specified list, you may also test if our child dictionary does exist inside the main dictionary. Below there are 2 sub-dictionaries "girls" and "Boys", we want to see if the Boys exists in our main dictionary "Dict" or not. So, we used the for loop with the if-else method.

```
Dict = {'Tim': 18,'Charlie':12,'Tiffany':22,'Robert':25}
Boys = {'Tim': 18,'Charlie':12,'Robert':25}
Girls = {'Tiffany':22}
for key in list(Dict.keys()):
    if key in list(Boys.keys()):
        print(True)
    else:
        print(False)
```

The for loop of the code checks every key inside the main dict for Boys keys.

If there is a boy key in the main dictionary, it will print true and if there isn't it will print false. The code, when executed, will output "True" 3 times since we have 3 elements in the "Boys" dictionary. This indicates that elements of "Boys" exist in Dict, the main dictionary.

Merging Dictionaries

The update () function will merge one dictionary to another. In the below code, we will merge the two dictionaries using update.

```
my_dict1 = {"username": "XYZ", "email": "xyz@gmail.com", "location":"Mumbai"}

my_dict2 = {"firstName" : "Nick", "lastName": "Price"}

my_dict1.update(my_dict2)

print(my_dict1)
```

Output:

```
{'username': 'XYZ', 'email': 'xyz@gmail.com', 'location': 'Mumbai', 'firstName':
'Nick', 'lastName': 'Price'}
```

Testing membership task

You can check if a key is present in a dictionary or otherwise. This examination can only be done on a dictionary's key and not the value. The "in" keyword is used to perform the affiliation evaluation. When you use the "in" keyword to search the key in the dictionary, the statement returns true or false.

On a dictionary, here's an example of a membership evaluation.

```
my_dict = {"username": "XYZ", "email": "xyz@gmail.com", "location":"Mumbai"}
print("email" in my_dict)
print("location" in my_dict)
print("test" in my_dict)
```

Output:

```
True
True
False
```

Appending Elements

Append () can be used to add elements to a dictionary. We just need to specify the key where we want to append.

```
my_dict = {"Name":[],"Address":[],"Age":[]};

my_dict["Name"].append("Guru")
my_dict["Address"].append("Mumbai")
my_dict["Age"].append(30)
print(my_dict)
```

Running this code will give the following output:

```
{'Name': ['Guru'], 'Address': ['Mumbai'], 'Age': [30]}
```

Accessing elements

The elements in dictionaries are key-value paired. To access elements, you have to specify the key.

```
my_dict = {"username": "XYZ", "email": "xyz@gmail.com", "location":"Mumbai"}
print("username :", my_dict['username'])
print("email : ", my_dict["email"])
print("location : ", my_dict["location"])
```

Output:

```
username : XYZ
email :  xyz@gmail.com
location :  Mumbai
```

Trying to access keys that don't exist will give errors.

Deleting Elements

Specific dictionary elements can be deleted using del.

```
del dict['yourkey']  # This will remove the element with your key.
```

To   delete   the   entire   dictionary:

```
del my_dict  # this will delete the dictionary with name my_dict
```

To empty the dictionary and clear the contents, we use clear:

```
your_dict.clear()
```

We can also delete elements using the pop keyword. How is this different? It returns the value of the element after deleting.

Adding and updating elements

```python
my_dict = {"username": "XYZ", "email": "xyz@gmail.com", "location":"Mumbai"}

my_dict['name']='Nick'

print(my_dict)
```

Output:

```
{'username': 'XYZ', 'email': 'xyz@gmail.com', 'location': 'Mumbai', 'name': 'Nic
k'}
```

If the key already exists then the value will be overwritten and hence updated.

4.4 Conditional Statements

These statements take your programming to the next level.

The if statement

You must already have some idea of what they do from the previous chapters. It has the basic form:

```python
if BOOLEAN EXPRESSION:
    STATEMENTS
```

Important points:

- The colon (:) is essential and necessary. It distinguishes the compound statement's header from the body.

- After the colon, the line should be indented. The usage of four spaces for indentation is common in Python.

- If BOOLEAN EXPRESSION is valid, all lines which are indented by the same amount afterward the colon would be run.

Take this example:

```
food = 'spam'

if food == 'spam':
    print('Ummmm, my favorite!')
    print('I feel like saying it 100 times...')
    print(100 * (food + '! '))
```

The condition is the Boolean expression that follows the if sentence. If this is true, all indented codes will be implemented. What if the situation isn't true, and food isn't the same as 'spam'? Nothing occurs in a basic if declaration like this, and the machine moves onto the following statement.

See what happens if you run this sample code. Then, instead of 'spam,' adjust the food to something else and run it again to make sure you don't get any result.

This flow chart will make it easier to understand:

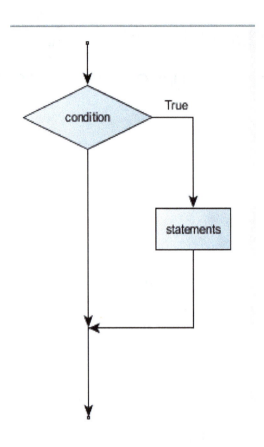

The if condition is a compound statement. A body and a header line make up compound statements. The if statement's header line starts with the term if, then a Boolean expression, and finally a colon (:).

A block refers to the indented sentences that follow. The block ends with the first sentence which is not indented. Each argument inside of the block must be indented in the same manner.

If else condition

While a situation is valid, you usually need one event to happen, and when it is wrong, you usually want something different to happen. The if-else condition is used to do this.

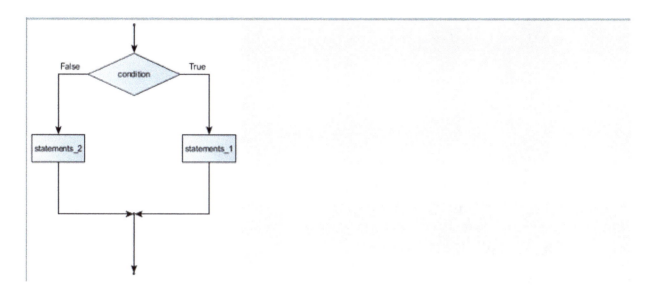

The basic syntax looks like this:

```
if BOOLEAN EXPRESSION:
    STATEMENTS_1         # executed if condition evaluates to True
else:
    STATEMENTS_2         # executed if condition evaluates to False
```

If a Boolean expression statement is True, each argument within the if block of the if-else line is performed in sequence. If the Boolean expression condition is False, the whole set of statements is ignored, but all the codes in the else section are implemented instead.

There is no restriction on how many statements may exist within the two lines of an if-else declaration, although each block must have at least one clause. A segment with no statements is sometimes useful (usually as a position holder or scaffolding for coding you have not written yet). In any scenario, the pass expression, which does little but function as a buffer, may be used.

```python
if True:          # This is always true
    pass          # so this is always executed, but it does nothing
else:
    pass
```

Sometimes there may be more than 2 possibilities. In that case, we chain the conditions.

```python
if x < y:
    STATEMENTS_A
elif x > y:
    STATEMENTS_B
else:
    STATEMENTS_C
```

The flowchart will look like this:

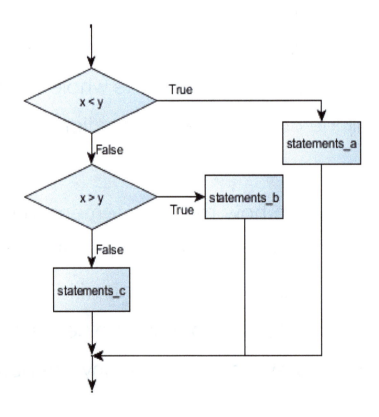

Elif is an acronym for else if. Just one branch would be executed. There is no restriction on the amount of elif statements that can be used, although only one (optional) final else argument can be used, and it has to be in the statement's last branch.

Each condition is examined one by one. If the 1st is incorrect, the 2nd is investigated, and so on. When one of them is valid, the sentence concludes with the execution of the corresponding section. Only the first valid branch is executed, even if there are multiple true conditions.

We can even nest if statements within another if statement. Something like this:

```
if x < y:
    STATEMENTS_A
else:
    if x > y:
        STATEMENTS_B
    else:
        STATEMENTS_C
```

4.5 Loops

Loops are useful in Python and other programming languages since they enable you to replay a section of code. You'll always find yourself in cases where you'll need to use a section of data repeatedly but don't want to compose the same piece of code twice.

The While Loop

When you first start learning how to code, among the first loops you'll possibly experience is the "while loop." This is also one of the easiest to grasp: once you consider the name of the loop, you'll soon realize that the term "while" is about "interval" or "time span." The term "loop" applies to a line of code that is executed frequently, as you might already understand.

With all this in view, the following description of the while loop should be clear:

A while loop is a computing term that, when used, repeats the execution of a code block while a specified condition remains valid.

While is a keyword that denotes a state that may be either False or True. Also, a code block that you like to run repeatedly.

That's what there is to it!

Here is an example to get you started:

```python
# Take user input
number = 2


# Condition of the while loop
while number < 5 :
    print("Thank you")
    # Increment the value of the variable "number by 1"
    number = number+1
```

Output:

```
Thank you
Thank you
Thank you
```

The while loop in the code illustration above is quite simple: When you wonder about it, the 3 elements you heard about earlier are all evident: the while keyword, accompanied by a state that is either False or True (number < 5) as well as a code block that you wish to run over and over again:

If you look closely at the above program, you'll see that there's a variable number inside which an integer 2 is stored. When the number's value is less than 5, they print "Thank you" and raise the number's valuation by one. While the number remains less than 5, Python continues to execute the following two code lines inside the while loop.

Before the number value equals 5 and the situation no longer evaluates to True, Python prints "Thank you" 2 more times. Since the state now becomes False, you'll leave the while loop and proceed with the rest of the code. There is no further programming in this situation, so the application can terminate.

This program was a little simple. Let's make it a bit more complex by adding conditionals:

```python
# Take user input
number = 2


# Condition of the while loop
while number < 5 :
    # Find the mod of 2
    if number%2 == 0:
        print("The number "+str(number)+" is even")
    else:
        print("The number "+str(number)+" is odd")


    # Increment `number` by 1
    number = number+1
```

Output:

```
The number 2 is even
The number 3 is odd
The number 4 is even
```

For Loops

The for loop may be approached in the same manner as the while loop. The "for" part of "for loop" applies to something which you repeat for a specific number of occasions, as you would assume.

If you remember all of the above, the for loop can be conveniently described as follows:

It is a coding concept that, when applied, repeats a bit of code "for" a predetermined number of times.

Unlike while loop, there is no active condition - you simply run a piece of code continuously for a number of periods. To put it another way, the while loop runs the code block within it only until the condition is True, whereas the for loop runs the code embedded in it for a certain number of occasions. A series or an arranged list of objects determines the "amount of times."

A for loop consists of

- The for keyword

- Followed by a variable

- The keyword in

- The built-in range() function to make a sequence of number

- Code that you want to execute

Here is an example:

```python
# Print "Thank you" 5 times
for number in range(5):
    print("Thank you")
```

Output:

```
Thank you
Thank you
Thank you
Thank you
Thank you
```

As you may be able to tell, the components that were introduced in the above part are shown in this small for loop example: the keyword "for", the "number" variable, the keyword "in", the range () function along with the code statements that you wish to execute repeatedly to print "Thankyou".

This looks so easy. And it is.

Look at this other example in which we use 2 variables. Recall the len built-in function which returns the length of a list.

```python
languages = ['R', 'Python', 'Scala', 'Java', 'Julia']

for index in range(len(languages)):
    print('Current language:', languages[index])
```

Output:

```
Current language: R
Current language: Python
Current language: Scala
Current language: Java
Current language: Julia
```

As you see, the for keyword is used to launch the loop. To generate a series of numbers, you just use variables languages and index, the keyword "in", and the range () feature. You will also see that the len () feature is used in this situation since the languages list isn't numerical. A print sentence is the code you would like to run repeatedly.

You mean to say in the loop earlier that you'd like to display the data science programming language for each index in the range of len (languages). Since len (languages) is now 5, the sentence may be rewritten as follows:

```
for index in range(5):
    print('Current language:', languages[index])
```

Changing this will get you the exact same result!

Nested Loops

You can customize your loops using conditional statements and you can even nest loops inside loops! Look at the example below:

```python
# Print the below statement 3 times
for number in range(3) :
    print("---------------------------------------")
    print("I am outer loop iteration "+str(number))
    # Inner loop
    for another_number in range(5):
        print("****************************")
        print("I am inner loop iteration "+str(another_number))
```

You'll see that the control joins the first loop and the variable number's value is set to 0. The first print command is executed, and control then moves to the second loop and sets the value of "another number" to 0. In the second loop, the first print code is only executed once.

The control now moves back to the inner loop, where the "another number" value is reset to the next integer, and the expression is printed using the print () method.

The preceding procedure proceeds until the control reaches the end of the range() method, which for this situation is 5, at which point it switches to the outer loop, initializes the number of the variable to the next integer, outputs the expression within the print() function, enters the inside loop, and performs the preceding steps till the range() is traversed.

This trip of the control between loops proceeds till the control has crossed the whole range, which in this situation is three times.

Chapter 5- Mistakes to Avoid with Python

These are a few of the most common Python mistakes. Be sure to avoid them.

1. Iterators are not used.

This is something that many Python newbies do, irrespective of their experience with other coding languages. There really is no way around it.

How can you use a for-loop for reaching items in a variable called list_ one after the other? We understand that lists are indexed, so we can use the list [i] to get to the i-th item. Using the for-loop, we can construct an iterator of integers ranging from zero to len (list_), as seen below:

```
for i in range(len(list_)):
    foo(list_[i])
```

It's efficient. The codes are in perfect working order. In other languages, as with C, this is often the normal way to create a for-loop. In Python, though, we can potentially do better.

How can you do it?

Are you aware that Python lists are iterable? By exploiting its iterable existence, we can generate even more simple codes, as seen below:

```
for element in list_:
    foo(element)
```

The zip function will traverse several lists in parallel in a for-loop, while the enumerate function can be useful if you focus on having the index number (namely the counter) when iterating over an iterable variable.

2. Use of global variables

A global variable is one that has a global scope and is defined in the main script, while a local variable is one that has a local scope and is declared inside a function. In Python, the global keyword helps you to view and modify global variables from inside a function. Here's an illustration:

Many beginners like it because it appears to get you out of having to move any of the arguments of the function. However, this is not the case. It merely conceals the acts.

Using global variables is often inefficient for debugging. Functions must be reusable and handled like block boxes. Functions that change global variables can have unintended consequences in the main scripts which are hard to detect, resulting in complicated code which is hard to debug.

It's a bad programming technique to change global variables inside a local function. The variable must be passed in as an argument, modified, and returned at the end of the function.

*Be careful not to mix up global variables and global constants, since the latter is entirely acceptable in most cases.

3. Not grasping the concept of mutable objects

Mutable objects, maybe the most frequent shock for novice Python users, since this function is exclusive to Python.

In Python, there are two types of objects. During runtime, mutable objects may modify their contents or states, while immutable objects cant. Many object types which are built-in, such as int, bool, float, and tuple, are immutable.

```
st = 'A string'
st[0] = 'B' # You cannot do this in Python
```

Data forms like set, list , and dict, from the other side, are mutable. So, for example, list [0] = 'fresh' may be used to modify the elements of elements inside a list.

The surprising happens when default arguments of functions are mutable. Consider the below function, where the default value of the list is a mutable empty list.

```python
def foo(element, list_=[]):
    list_.append(element)
    return list_
```

Let us call the function two times without passing an argument to list_ to force it to use the default value. If a 2nd argument isn't given, a new empty list should be generated any time the feature is called.

```python
a = foo(1) # returns [1]
b = foo(2) # returns [1,2], not [2]! WHY?
```

WHY IS THIS THE CASE?

In python, default arguments are only evaluated once, during the definition of the function. This ensures that calling it would not cause the default arguments to be refreshed.

As a result, if the default statement is mutable, it will be changed each time the functions are called. Any subsequent function calls will use the default argument which is mutated. The 'basic' solution is to set the default to (immutable) None, as seen below.

```
def foo(element, list_=None):
    if list_ is None:
        list_ = []
    list_.append(element)
    return list_
```

4. Avoiding to copy

For certain learners, the idea of copying can be unfamiliar or perhaps counterintuitive. Consider the following scenario: we get a list c = [[1,3],[4,6]], and we make a newer list b = c. There are currently two lists of the same components in them. Isn't it true that modifying certain components in list b has no impact on list c?

That's incorrect.

```
a = [[0,1],[2,3]]
b = a

b[1][1] = 100

print(a,b)
# [[0, 1], [2, 100]] [[0, 1], [2, 100]]
print(id(a)==id(b))
# True
```

All changes made to the items of one list are apparent in both if you 'copy' a list by using assignment expression, i.e. b = c Since the assignment operator only generates links between an object and a target, all lists b and a in the example have the same relation, which in Python is id().

How do I make copies of objects?

There are two approaches for creating copies if you wish to 'clone' artifacts and then change the elements in the current (or previous) object without changing the bindings: deep copy and shallow copy. The references of two things would be different.

You may make a shallow copy for c by using b = copy.copy(c) . A shallow copy produces a newer object that contains the initial elements' references. This can seem to be difficult, but consider the below example:

```
import copy

a = [[0,1],[2,3]]
b = copy.copy(a)

print(id(a)==id(b))
# False

b[1] = 100
print(a,b)
# [[0, 1], [2, 3]] [[0, 1], 100]

b[0][0] = -999
print(a,b)
# [[-999, 1], [2, 3]] [[-999, 1], 100]
print(id(a[0]) == id(b[0]))
# True
```

As soon as a shallow copy of nested list c is made, which we name b, 2 lists have unique references id(c) != id(b), the sign != means 'not equal'. But, the elements they have, have similar references, and so id(c[0]) == id(b[0]).

This implies that modifying the elements in b has little effect on list c, but modifying the elements in b[1] has an impact on c[1], so this is a shallow

In other words, if b would be a shallow duplicate of c, any modifications made to elements inside nested items in b would show in c.

A deep copy of c by b = copy.deepcopy(c) is needed if you desire to copy an object which is nested with no bindings between its components. A deep copy generates a new entity and clones nested items in the initial elements recursively.

Deep copy, in a nutshell, clones everything with no bindings.

There you have it: four basic Python novice errors to stop. You don't have to master them the difficult way as I did.

Conclusion

There you have it. We have discussed the fundamentals of Python programming. With this knowledge, you can start your journey into the coding world!

Python is a vast programming knowledge and you have just scratched the surface with this book. This book has given you the tools to venture into Python. The most important thing with any skill is practice. I advise you to practice the concepts in this book yourself, as much as you can. Along with that also experiment and try new stuff.

When you feel that you have mastered the basics of this book then venture on to learn new things. There is a lot we haven't taught like declaring your own functions or taking inputs. Rest assured that learning those new concepts will be a piece of cake after you have properly absorbed the knowledge in this book.

I hope this book has ignited your passion for programming and I am sure it will help you in many aspects of life.